Norton

The Loveable Cat Who Travelled the World

PETER GETHERS

Adapted for young readers
by Ruth Knowles

Norton: The Loveable Cat Who Travelled the World
A RED FOX BOOK 978 1 849 41387 9

Published in Great Britain by Red Fox Books,
an imprint of Random House Children's Books
A Random House Group Company

This edition published 2010

1 3 5 7 9 10 8 6 4 2

The Random House Group Limited supports the Forest Stewardship
Council (FSC), the leading international forest certification organization.
All our titles that are printed on Greenpeace-approved FSC-certified
paper carry the FSC logo. Our paper procurement policy can be found
at www.rbooks.co.uk/environment.

Mixed Sources
Product group from well-managed
forests and other controlled sources
www.fsc.org   Cert no. TT-COC-2139
© 1996 Forest Stewardship Council

Typeset in 13/20 Garamond by Falcon Oast Graphic Art Ltd.

Red Fox Books are published by Random House Children's Books,
61–63 Uxbridge Road, London W5 5SA

Addre... ...nited

TH... ...9

A CIP ca... ...ibrary.

Printed and... ...R0 4TD

Dear Reader,

This is a book about an extraordinary cat. I never thought I would ever write a book about a cat. In fact I never thought I would even own a cat. Amazingly enough I used to hate cats! But then I met Norton and my life changed.

Ever since he was a tiny kitten, Norton automatically went where I went – on holiday, out for dinner, to my office . . . He has eaten in great restaurants, gone on boats, trains and planes, stayed in fancy hotels, gone for long walks with me – without a leash!

I love my cat. And I have never heard of any other cat quite like him. This is his story. I hope you enjoy it . . .

Peter

Norton

The Loveable Cat Who Travelled the World

CONTENTS

"Who's He For?"   1

Where to Sleep . . . ?   9

Travelling By Pocket   15

Going On Holiday!   23

Exploring   31

Solo Stroll   39

Fighting With Sand   47

"Get Him Out Of Here!"   55

Norton Tries To Make Friends   63

Surprising Dad   71

Playing In The Snow   77

The Guest Of Honour In Paris   85

Moving On   95

"Norton! Norton!"   103

CHAPTER ONE

"Who's He For?"

Ring, ring! Ring, ring! The noise of the telephone sounded through Peter Gethers's New York flat, making him jump. He quickly put down his book, pushed his glasses up onto his head and went to answer it. "Hello?"

He grinned to himself as soon as he heard the voice on the other end. "I'm at the airport!" said his girlfriend, Cindy. "Are you awake?"

"I'm awake," Peter told her. "See you soon."

Cindy had been away for a few days visiting her family. He did enjoy being by himself, able to do whatever he wanted, whenever he wanted – but he had missed her. Still smiling, he put down the phone

1

and went back to his book. Soon he was lost in it again.

Half an hour later, Peter heard the door to his flat open. He ran a hand through his brown hair to try and neaten it up and then went to greet his girlfriend. "I—"

But before he could even finish his first word, Cindy interrupted him: "I've got something to show you." She was laughing with excitement. "Stay there. Close your eyes and I'll tell you when to open them."

Puzzled, Peter did as he was told. *What* has *she bought me?* he wondered.

"OK! Open them," called Cindy. Peter thought she sounded a little nervous now.

He opened his eyes.

Then he closed them for a moment before opening them again.

Cindy was holding something out in her hands, but Peter had absolutely no idea what it was. He took a step towards her and squinted down at the tiny thing. He wondered if it could be a mouse, but as Cindy moved closer, he realized — to his surprise — that it was a cat. A very small grey cat, with strange-looking ears, blue eyes and a round head.

The kitten was sitting up on Cindy's palm now, swivelling his little head about inquisitively and trying to take in all the new things around him.

Peter was amazed; Cindy hadn't mentioned that she was getting a pet. "Who's he for?" he asked.

There was silence. Peter frowned. What had Cindy done? Had she bought this ball of grey fluff for *him*? She knew he hated cats. If he ever decided to get a pet, he wanted a dog — a dog called Norton — a dog that he would choose for himself, thank you very much.

He opened his mouth. *Who's he for?* he wanted to ask Cindy again, but suddenly the kitten seemed to answer his question: he stopped moving his head about, stared straight into Peter's eyes and mewed softly. The corners of his mouth turned up — and Peter was suddenly convinced that the little cat was smiling at him.

He couldn't help but smile back.

Cindy smiled too. Then she broke the silence and nodded. "He's yours."

Peter wasn't quite sure what to do or how to behave now. He had simply been expecting Cindy home from California, not Cindy plus a kitten – even if it was a very cute kitten. Peter didn't really know why she had bought him this creature – but for now, that didn't matter. This little guy had melted his heart. It was love at first sight.

Without saying anything more, Cindy held out her hand towards Peter, and he moved closer. He had never had anything to do with a baby of any kind before, so he wasn't really sure how to handle it. He decided to just trust his instincts. Gently, he picked up the kitten and held him up to his face so that they were nose to nose. Now, for the first time, Peter could take a proper look at his new companion.

"He's a Scottish Fold and he's six weeks old," Cindy told him as he and his new pet stared at each other intently. "There's something very special about him. I don't think he's just a normal cat. He seems so intelligent."

Peter couldn't believe how much his own feelings could change in such a short amount of time. If Cindy had asked him earlier in the day whether he wanted a cat, his answer would have been a very firm "No"! Now, thanks to this fluffy grey bundle in front of him, he felt totally different. It was as if this beautiful kitten with the weird ears belonged here with him in this flat. He swapped the kitten from one hand to the other, then ran his hand lightly over the tiny body, stroking the soft, smooth fur. "Of course he's not just a normal cat," Peter told Cindy. "He's mine!"

Norton at six weeks old:	
Weight	less than 1kg
Length	About 15cm
Appearance	Like all Scottish Folds, he has folded-down ears and blue eyes. Light grey in colour, with a few patches of darker grey. White paws, and white ring around his nose. Very bushy tail.

The kitten began to wriggle about, as if he wanted to get down, so Peter carefully bent and set him on the floor.

"He'll be scared," Cindy warned. "Kittens are always frightened of new surroundings."

But this kitten was proving her quite wrong! Very casually, he padded over to one of the sofas in Peter's living room, then across to the opposite one; next he came back to a spot in between the two, plopped down on a rug and fell asleep.

Peter heard contented purrs and watched as the kitten's chest moved rhythmically up and down. He couldn't stop the grin spreading across his face. Suddenly, as he watched this tiny sleeping ball of fur that was now his, a name came to him. Why wait for a dog he might or might not get when this perfect little creature was here in front of him? "Norton," he called softly. "Norton . . ."

The kitten's eyes opened to narrow slits, then a little bit more, then still more – until finally he was looking straight at Peter. It was as if he understood that he had just heard his own name for the first time.

"Look," Peter cried. "He already knows his name!"

Norton was home.

CHAPTER TWO

Where to Sleep ...?

Scottish Fold cats:

- Their ears fold over in half, forward and then down, giving them what is often known as an 'owl-like' appearance.
- They have rounder heads than other breeds.
- They have short, firm, trim bodies.
- They do come from Scotland: the original Scottish Fold was discovered in 1961 at a farm near Dundee. She was called Susie.

For a long time after Cindy had left, Peter sat watching his snoozing pet, but when at last he realized that it was time for him to go to bed himself, he wasn't sure what to do with Norton. He was reluctant to disturb him – he'd had a long journey from California, and had then been introduced to his new home and his new master, so Peter thought he probably deserved the rest. But what if he woke up during the night and didn't know where he was?

Peter was so completely unprepared for looking after a cat that he didn't even know where Norton *should* sleep: not with him in his bed, surely . . . ? What if the cat wriggled about all night, keeping him awake? Norton would probably be scared in his big bed anyway. Waking up next to a grown man he'd only met the day before might be terrifying for the kitten.

Unable to come up with a better solution, Peter just decided to leave Norton where he was. If he wasn't comfortable and wanted to find somewhere else to doze, he could choose.

And he did!

Peter got ready for bed and snuggled under the sheets. He was just drifting off to sleep when he heard a scratching noise from the living room. It sounded as if Norton was sliding around on the floor, but it stopped before Peter had chance to go and investigate, so he assumed the kitten had gone back to sleep. Soon, he did the same himself . . .

The next morning when Peter woke, he knew that something amazing had happened, but it took him a while to wake up properly and remember what it was. *Norton!* He suddenly remembered that he now had a gorgeous Scottish Fold kitten.

Lying there, Peter listened out for the slipping and sliding he'd heard from the living room the night before. Silence. Maybe Norton was still sleeping. But if so, he'd been asleep for an awfully long time. Peter opened his eyes fully. Why wasn't Norton making any noise? Was he already in trouble?

Peter started to stir. *I'd better go and investigate*, he thought to himself. But just as he was about to get out of bed, he felt something move by his head. He turned to see – very, very close to him on the pillow – a tiny grey ball of fluff. Norton was lying peacefully just next to Peter's head. His intelligent blue eyes were wide open, but he wasn't moving at all; he just stared intently at his new master. It was as though he was just waiting to see what Peter did before he decided whether to follow him.

Peter couldn't believe it. Norton hadn't even lived in this flat or known Peter for a day, and yet he already felt happy and comfortable enough to sleep next to him. Surely that meant he liked it and felt happy and safe here already? Peter didn't want to spoil the moment, so, trying not to move his head, he reached round with his arm and gently stroked Norton, first rubbing the top of his head, then between his eyes, and then all the way down to his soft little nose.

Norton purred contentedly; he shifted about and, knowing exactly what he wanted, stretched his head up so that Peter was able to scratch under his chin. It looked like he had already decided that he and Peter were going to be the best of friends!

* * *

They spent the day happily getting to know each other. Then, the next night, the same thing happened. Norton started out sleeping peacefully on the living-room floor, but as soon as Peter had fallen asleep he padded gently into his new master's bedroom, hopped onto the bed and snuggled up into his neck.

Peter woke the following morning to find Norton lying peacefully on the pillow, once again staring intently at him. As soon as Peter had given his cat another morning stroke, and Norton had meowed his thanks, they headed for the kitchen together. Peter gave Norton a tin of cat food – chicken in cream sauce – while he sipped some coffee, and they enjoyed their breakfast together in happy silence.

That night, Peter was expecting to fall asleep alone, and then wake up to find Norton beside him again, but the little kitten had other ideas. Obviously feeling very settled in his new environment, and realizing that Peter enjoyed having him snuggled up next to him, the little cat trotted in the moment his owner got into bed and jumped up next to him. Peter made some space beside him on the pillow and Norton curled up into it. Then, both breathing heavily and contentedly, they went to sleep.

CHAPTER THREE

Travelling By Pocket!

By the end of Norton's first week in New York, Peter was beginning to think that his new pet should see some of the city he now lived in – in fact, anything that was outside the four walls of his flat. Secretly he also wanted to show his gorgeous, friendly, well-behaved little kitten off to people!

Norton had settled into Peter's flat very easily and happily; he had clearly trusted and loved Peter – and Cindy – from the moment they met. Peter was sure the little kitten would be fine travelling around with him, so he decided to take him over to visit one of his friends who had a cat of her own – he thought it would do Norton good to meet a fellow feline.

But his friend was concerned. "Will he be OK?" she asked. "Norton is only little, after all. I don't want my cat to scare him."

Peter couldn't see how anything or anybody could object to Norton. "We're coming over!" he told her.

It was a grey day, threatening rain, so Peter put on his raincoat. Once he had it on, he realized it had very big pockets – more than big enough for a seven-week-old Scottish Fold kitten! So he popped Norton in a pocket and they left the flat together.

Norton barely reacted; he simply sat calmly inside Peter's coat. He seemed very happy in there, only stirring every so often as Peter walked along to stick out his head and have a look at his surroundings before snuggling back inside again.

When they arrived, Peter soon saw that he had been right. Norton was just as confident in a stranger's house as he was in his own new home. Peter gently lifted the kitten out of his pocket and set him down in the hallway of his friend's flat. Norton sniffed around, a little unsure of his surroundings at first, but then padded off to explore, prowling from room to room.

The house cat suddenly emerged, having sniffed out this little grey intruder, and interrupted Norton's wanderings. The moment he spotted him in *his* living room, he hissed loudly and circled Norton, ready for a challenge, the hairs on his back sticking up like a brush. Peter held his breath. Next to this big tabby, Norton looked absolutely tiny; he was completely vulnerable. But Norton held his own. He lifted his head, and stared straight into the face of the strange cat as if to say, *Who are you kidding?* Then he lay down on the floor and rolled over, looking as cute and as fluffy as he possibly could! The adult cat hesitated for a moment, but then realized he had no option but to be friendly to Norton so that his owner didn't tell him off.

In a matter of minutes, Norton had totally won him over: he had made his first feline friend!

Over the next few days and weeks, Norton often travelled around in the same way – in a coat of Peter's that happened to have big, deep pockets. And Peter quickly got used to walking around New York with one hand in his pocket so he could stroke Norton. He realized that he could rely on his kitten to stay put. He never tried to jump out and run off. He was just interested in seeing new places and things, and he wanted to see them with Peter. Soon the two felt confident enough to travel like this on public transport too – and Norton loved it!

One Saturday morning they took the train to go and do some of Peter's errands. Norton loved the stopping and starting of the train and kept poking out first his nose and then the rest of his head to have a look around, before settling down again. Quite a few of the other passengers caught sight of the funny little kitten, then turned to their companions to smile and comment on how cute he was. Peter felt very proud!

Wherever they went, the praise of Norton continued. As soon as a tiny nose popped out of Peter's pocket, somebody would say "*Ahh!*" and come over to investigate. As soon as he stuck his head out, the cooing grew even louder, and everyone made a big fuss of the kitten. After a visit to the bakery, he left with some scraps of jam doughnuts and cookies; in the grocery shop he was given some cheese and chicken as a treat, which he golloped down happily. He loved his life in New York!

Peter worked part time for a big book-publishing company; he was also a writer himself, so he was often at home during the day, which meant that he and Norton could spend lots of time together. And if Peter was just popping out for something, he would always take his kitten with him.

Whenever Peter did go anywhere without Norton, and was absent for a while, he would return to find his pet pacing up and down by the door. Cindy had bought Peter a book about looking after cats, and when he consulted it, he was shocked. He learned that Norton was very likely worried sick about him. All cats still have jungle instincts left over from their days in the wild. So whenever Peter was late home, Norton would be wondering if his master had been attacked and eaten while he was out, leaving him abandoned.

> **Domestic cats like Norton are thought to originate from the African Wildcat, so there are similarities in their behaviour:**
> - Cats have well-developed senses
> - They are great hunters
> - They are very fast and agile
> - They communicate in lots of different ways
> - They are very independent
> - They are meat eaters
> - They love sleep so that they have enough energy
> - They are playful
> - They are clean

After learning this, Peter decided to take Norton with him whenever and wherever he possibly could. He didn't want to stress his cat out – and he did love having him with him, after all.

"You can't take your cat on trips all over the place," Cindy told him.

"Why not?" asked Peter. Surely Norton would be happier coming with him than hanging around the flat worrying all day? Peter was sure it would work.

Some weeks later, however, he had to go for a lunch meeting in a smart restaurant, so he put on his coat and headed for the door alone. Norton assumed they were going somewhere together and trotted over, ready to be lifted into Peter's pocket.

Instead, Peter bent down to stroke his soft fur. "Not today, little man. You'll have to stay here." He started to leave, but when he turned back for a last look at Norton, he found he couldn't do it. The little cat's face looked so sad. "I'm going to a fancy restaurant, Norton," he tried to explain. But Norton went on staring at him and meowed pitifully.

Peter just couldn't resist him, so he scooped him up and put him in his pocket. Off they headed together as usual!

And he needn't have worried: Norton stayed quietly in Peter's pocket for the whole meal. About halfway through, Peter thought the little cat might need some refreshment, so he sneaked him out of his pocket and set him gently down underneath his chair. Then he caught the attention of a waitress. "Could I have a glass of water, and also some milk – the milk in a short, round glass, please?" he asked. The poor waitress looked puzzled, but did as she was asked.

When she returned with the drinks, Peter set the milk under his chair for Norton. Immediately he heard the sound of Norton's tongue, swirling around like a little machine, furiously lapping at the milk.

When lunch was over and Peter got up to leave, he bent down to scoop up Norton and the now-empty glass. Just before they left the restaurant, Peter glanced back at his seat. *Oops!* Norton was a very messy drinker, and now there was a puddle of milk under the chair. Peter grinned to himself, and wondered what on earth the waitress would think he'd been up to!

CHAPTER FOUR

Going On Holiday!

When he visited restaurants or went on train journeys with Peter, Norton usually showed how trustworthy and well-behaved he was. But there were also times when it was clear that he had a rebellious streak!

One evening, Peter and Cindy were watching the television together. Suddenly Cindy sat up and looked around. Peter glanced at her for a second or two, frowning, but then he too heard the strange noise that had caught her attention.

"*Nooo!*" Cindy shrieked.

Peter looked down in the direction she was pointing – there was Norton, scratching the side of the sofa, the material slowly being destroyed by his claws.

"What's wrong?" Peter asked his girlfriend. He'd actually caught Norton doing this before – it was something the little cat obviously loved, so Peter hadn't been able to bring himself to reprimand him for it. "It's only a couch," he told Cindy.

But Cindy clearly didn't feel the same way. "You can't raise a kitten like that," she said firmly. "You need to be the one to teach him the difference between right and wrong." And in her eyes, at least, wrecking expensive furniture was wrong.

Peter realized that if he took Norton over to a friend's house and he decided to attack their sofa, they might not be too pleased, so he decided to listen to her.

He bent down towards Norton. "No," he told him in a firm voice. Norton was clever – Peter had realized that from the moment they met, and the cat didn't let him down now. Realizing that Peter's voice was different from usual, he immediately lifted his head, stopped what he was doing and moved away from the sofa.

Good! Peter settled back down in his seat to carry on watching the television . . .

But cheeky Norton wasn't quite ready to give up his favourite hobby. He kept eye contact with Peter and slunk back towards the sofa. Then, just a second later, he began scratching it again.

'No!' Peter said again, clapping his hands this time. Norton scampered away and plopped down on the floor. Satisfied that Norton had now definitely given up, Peter was soon involved in the television programme again.

Two minutes later, however, Cindy nudged him and looked down at the sofa leg again, shaking her head. Peter couldn't believe it – there was Norton, scratching away at the material once more. Peter wasn't happy at having to replace his furniture, but he was secretly impressed with his cat's cheekiness!

Every so often, Cindy would complain that she was beginning to feel a bit left out these days: Peter was spending a great deal of time with his new kitten. However, she also saw how well the two of them were getting on, and how happy they made each other, so one day she went out and got herself a little cat too!

Peter was introduced to her new kitten that very same day. He was very sweet, and so handsome – with a beautiful dark coat that had streaks of black and brown in it. Cindy named him Marlowe. He could jump much higher than Norton, but for Peter this was the only thing about him that *was* better: Norton was by far the cuter cat!

Marlowe arrived just when Peter was planning to take Norton on a trip out of New York. Every summer he usually spent his weekends on an island, in a little house by the beach in a town called Fair Harbour. It was a quiet, peaceful place with only one restaurant and two shops – and no cars, which meant it would be perfect – and a very safe spot for Norton to visit on his first trip out of New York. Peter loved it, and he hoped Norton would too.

Cindy and Marlowe decided they were going

to come too, so now they just had the challenge of getting out there!

As both cats were still so little, Peter and Cindy decided they would put them together in one travel case for the journey. But looking at them in there before the minibus arrived, Peter felt terrible. Was it really comfortable to travel like this? They didn't seem to have any other choice – they had to get the cats there safely, after all.

After the minibus had been going for about fifteen minutes, Peter wanted to check that the small creatures were OK, so he opened the case a little and stuck his hand in to stroke them. Marlowe took no notice of him at all and stayed where he was, in the back corner of the case, but Norton immediately pushed his soft nose against Peter's hand and rubbed it gently.

He couldn't resist it! When Cindy wasn't looking, Peter reached in and gently lifted Norton out onto his lap. The kitten meowed gratefully and soon settled down.

It didn't take Cindy long to notice. She shook her head and rolled her eyes at Peter.

He tried to explain. "He looked so unhappy in there," he insisted.

But Cindy wasn't buying it! "He didn't look unhappy. You were unhappy because you weren't holding him."

And deep down, Peter knew she was right. He smiled down at Norton, who was now curled up like a fluffy grey ball, resting his head on the back of Peter's hand. He just felt better when Norton was close – and he knew the little cat felt the same.

As the taxi journey went on, Norton gradually pulled himself further and further up Peter's arm – he wanted a good view of everything that was flying by outside the window! The little cat finally found a comfortable position on Peter's shoulder. From there he could watch the countryside pass by. He wanted to take everything in and he hunched forward with his nose pressed against the window. Every so often he would turn and look at Peter, as if to say, *What's all this? Tell me, will you?* before turning back to the window so he didn't miss anything.

Soon, the other people in the taxi noticed that

Peter had company, and leaned over to pet Norton. The little cat seemed to love the attention and stayed perfectly still while he was cooed over and stroked, looking at his admirers with his beautiful blue eyes. Then he snuggled down on Peter's shoulder and went to sleep.

CHAPTER FIVE

Exploring

While Norton slept on Peter's shoulder, Marlowe had been snoozing in his little corner of the carry case, seemingly unbothered by his journey. But as soon as Peter and Cindy carried him onto the next stage of his journey, the ferry which would take them over to the island, things changed! Little Marlowe clearly didn't like being on the water one bit and he jerked about awkwardly in the case, meowing loudly.

Cindy put her hand in to try and comfort him, but he pulled away, almost as if he was annoyed with her for making him do this. He retreated into his corner, dark eyes alert, staring out.

In total contrast, Norton seemed to love the ferry

even more than the taxi. The little cat pushed his nose out through the bars of the case, his eyes looking about excitedly – he wanted to see everything! So once again, Peter found himself scooping Norton out and putting him on his knee.

But Norton suddenly decided that the view from Peter's lap was not good enough. He wanted to see the water! He started climbing up towards Peter's shoulder to take a proper look. Peter knew just how much Norton liked seeing new things, but he didn't plan on diving off the ferry to rescue him from the sea. Holding onto him very, very tightly, Peter lifted him up so that he could see over the side of the boat. Norton moved closer, putting his paws on the rails. Cindy was terrified that he would wriggle away and end up in the water, but Peter went along with him, trusting him not to do anything stupid.

Norton was in heaven! His mouth was turning up at the corners into a smile as he gazed at all the blue sea and the land in the distance. He couldn't wait to get there!

* * *

An hour later, Peter, Norton, Cindy and Marlowe arrived at the beach house. Peter and Cindy immediately flipped open the travel case so the kittens could get out, stretch and relax after their long, exciting journey. Marlowe stayed put in his corner, not sure what to make of his new surroundings, but Norton was out of there quick as a flash!

The little cat had padded round the whole house in a matter of minutes, inspecting everything carefully – sniffing all around the couch, then the kitchen. There were steps up to a loft section where the bedroom was and he climbed up there too. When he'd finished checking it out, he stood looking down, watching Peter and Cindy below him.

Suddenly Peter realized what the kitten was planning to do – he wanted to jump all the way back down to the living room instead of using the steps. It was a long way, and Peter couldn't bear the thought of him hurting himself, so he shook his head. For a moment it looked as though the rebellious, sofa-scratching Norton was about to go ahead and jump.

But finally, obediently, he came downstairs in the normal way. Peter sighed in relief.

The next room on Norton's list was the bathroom. But he'd only been in there a moment when Peter heard him crying out. Wondering if the door had shut and his kitten was stuck inside, Peter rushed over, but when he reached the bathroom, he burst out laughing at what he saw. Norton was stuck, but not in the way he'd expected: his odd little ears were peeking over the side of the bathtub. He had obviously jumped up onto the edge to have a look at it properly, but the ceramic sides were so slippery that he'd slid right down into the bath and now he couldn't climb out!

Norton immediately tried to reach his master, but as soon as his little paws tried to get a grip on the shiny sides, he simply slid all the way back down towards the plughole. After Norton had been through this process a few times, still mewing crossly, Peter took pity on the little fellow, reached in and lifted him out. He kissed Norton on the head and set him down on the floor again. The cat looked back at the bath in disgust, but then trotted off to continue his investigation of the new house.

With him now safely out of the bathroom, Peter and Cindy left Norton to carry on exploring and turned their attention to Marlowe. He was still in his carry case, not sure what to make of things.

"Come on, Marlowe. Come on, boy," Cindy said, reaching in to stroke him. Peter was standing watching them, when suddenly he heard a loud ripping noise. He and Cindy both turned in shock. There it was again. And again.

"Oh, no!" cried Cindy. Peter looked up to where she was now pointing. There were big, long, colourful pieces of material covering the walls in the living room. Right up near the top of one of them, hanging on by his claws, was Norton!

For a moment Peter just stood and marvelled. His little kitten had managed to climb all the way up there! But then there was another ripping sound and Peter realized that if he didn't stop Norton soon, he was going to end up having to replace every single piece of material in the beach house. "Come on, Norton. Down you come." He managed to coax Norton down so that he could scoop him up, saving the cloth from any more damage.

Peter decided to distract Norton with some food, and Cindy thought this might also be what Marlowe needed, so they quickly got out some bowls and filled them with food and water. Marlowe wasn't interested, and Norton took only a few nibbles before heading excitedly for the door.

Peter realized that his little cat just wanted to get out and explore Fair Harbour! But he was worried: Norton was only three months old, he'd never wandered about freely in New York, and although Peter knew he needed to experience the outdoors, he couldn't bring himself to just let his cat roam about alone.

Suddenly he had an idea. He put a blue collar on Norton and fetched a really, really long piece of string. Then he tied one end of the string to the collar and the other end to the front-door handle, and he and Cindy headed outside to sit on the porch.

Norton was so excited to be outside, he almost

didn't know what to do with himself. As soon as he stepped through the door, he got down into a crouch, glancing around nervously as if waiting for something to attack him. Next he took just a little step forward, sniffing about all the time, his bright eyes alert. His folded-up ears were twitching as he tried to take in all the new smells and sounds around him. He hesitated for a moment; then, giving Peter a quick look, as if to say, *Thank you*, he suddenly jumped high into the air and let out an excited meow, before taking off and running wildly round the patio.

Peter grinned. He knew he'd made the right decision. Norton was as happy as he'd ever seen him.

However, the cat didn't seem to realize that he was attached to the string and the string was attached to the door! After a few moments of running to and fro, the string was crisscrossing the porch in a tangled web, and Norton couldn't move a muscle. It ran under a chair, around the table, around another chair and twice around Cindy's ankles, then back around the chairs again! For now, Norton wasn't going anywhere, but Peter could see that it was only a matter of time before he set off on his adventures.

CHAPTER SIX

Solo Stroll

Norton loved his first weekend at Fair Harbour so much that they all went up there again the following one. And the next. And the next. And soon he and Peter and Cindy and Marlowe were visiting every single weekend.

On one occasion, Cindy and Marlowe had to stay in New York, so Norton and Peter headed down together, just the two of them – a boys-only trip! They were both looking forward to it. Norton was getting bigger all the time, and he now had his own travelling case. He barely needed it though: he sat quietly on Peter's knee for the journey in the minibus and the ferry.

He was so familiar with their trip by now that Peter thought he could probably get to Fair Harbour by himself! On the ferry, as Norton calmly and confidently took up his usual position, his little paws resting on the rails of the boat as he looked out to sea, Peter suddenly felt sure that he was ready to explore Fair Harbour alone – not attached to any string. The little cat was confident and relaxed there, and it seemed like the right time to give him some more independence. It was probably a good thing for the beach house too – the whole porch was so covered in string it looked like Peter had been playing a giant game of cat's cradle!

The next morning, Norton seemed to know that something big was going to happen. The moment he woke, he jumped out of bed and immediately padded over to the front door. He waited there impatiently, turning his head to see what was taking Peter so long. Hearing the impatient meows, Peter decided it was unfair to keep the little guy waiting any longer, and so, rubbing the sleep from his eyes, he quickly got dressed and headed for the front door too.

As his hand rested on the handle, Peter felt a sudden shiver of anxiety, but he knew he had to let Norton grow up . . . so he took a deep breath and opened the door. Norton wasted absolutely no time, rushing out happily into the sunshine. In the blink of an eye he was gone, a blur of grey, racing back and forth across the garden.

Peter wasn't quite ready to leave Norton completely alone. The kitten was obviously ecstatic at being let off the string, but he still looked so little and vulnerable, so Peter followed him to see what he was getting up to and check he was safe.

Norton was having the time of his life! He frolicked about, chasing birds and squirrels, crawling through the grass on his belly and chomping flowers. Watching him, Peter was reminded that his little domesticated pet cat was definitely related to bigger wild cats like lions: he moved like them now, a beast on the prowl.

After half an hour of watching him carefully, Peter decided it was safe to leave Norton to his own devices, and he headed indoors to have some breakfast and get started on his writing for the day. He wasn't *really* worried that Norton would stray too far from the house, but every so often he got up from his desk and went to check that the kitten was still in sight – just to be on the safe side! "Norton!" he called. And within seconds, he would hear Norton's happy meow, letting him know that he was safe and well and Peter could go back to work.

A few hours later, Peter's tummy started rumbling, distracting him. When he looked at his watch and saw that it was lunch time, he decided to head out to the shop to buy some food. He stood in the front doorway and watched Norton. The cat was still having so much fun playing that Peter decided to leave him behind. *I'll only be twenty minutes*, he thought to himself; Norton probably wouldn't even notice he was gone.

He started off, but he had only been walking for a couple of minutes when he heard a noise behind him. It sounded like a faint growling meow. He took another two steps. There was the sound again. Peter stopped and turned. On the pavement behind him was Norton! He had obviously been trying to follow Peter, but his little legs just couldn't keep up.

"What are you doing?" Peter asked his cat. "Go back to the house and play." And he turned to set off for the shop again.

But Norton obviously wasn't happy with this. There was an even louder meow. And when Peter turned again, he saw that Norton had scampered closer to him.

Thinking that his cat simply didn't want to be left alone, Peter bent down so he was on Norton's level. "Come on then. Let's go," he said, and waited for Norton to trot over and either climb onto his hand or into his pocket. But to his amazement, although Norton approached him, he stopped about a metre away.

"All right, then. I'll walk slowly," Peter told him, getting hungrier by the second.

But Norton stared at his master challengingly, stubbornly staying exactly where he was.

"OK. Have it your own way." Peter took a few more steps towards the shop, and then glanced back to see what his cat was doing now. He grinned to himself. Norton was following him, but stopped whenever he stopped. He wanted to keep Peter in sight, but he wanted to do this walk by himself!

So Peter walked on, with Norton following behind. Some people stopped and stared as this strange procession passed them, but Peter pretended he hadn't noticed and carried on as though there was absolutely nothing unusual about this situation.

Norton meowed every now and then, letting his owner know that he was still there, but he seemed to be enjoying his first solo stroll through Fair Harbour.

There was a moment when a motorbike zoomed by noisily: Peter turned to check Norton wasn't frightened by it – his little cat had never been so close to a vehicle like that before, and he froze for a moment, his blue eyes darting about, unsure what to do.

"It's OK, little guy," Peter reassured him. And once the bike had passed, Norton carried on as before, stubbornly keeping his distance from Peter the whole way to the shop!

Peter was so proud of his cat — he'd made it all the way here by himself! But on their arrival, Peter realized this might be a bit too much for his little cat to cope with. There were about ten times more people here than he had ever seen before in his whole life. Peter wondered whether it might be best to just scoop Norton up and put him in his pocket so he'd feel safe, but before he had chance to do this, Norton made up his own mind, and dived into a row of thick bushes nearby.

He had followed his master all the way into town so obediently that Peter assumed he just wanted a bit of peace and quiet — surely he'd stay in the bushes until Peter returned. He headed into the shop to buy his lunch.

But returning to the bush where Norton had been hiding a few minutes later, Peter was faced with a disaster. Norton was nowhere to be seen!

He stood there, calling his name . . . Nothing. Then he bent down and had a look inside the greenery. No sign of any grey fur at all. Peter felt sick and panicky; his heart was pounding and he was starting to sweat. How could he have been so stupid? Norton had never been outside the safety of the porch and the garden before, and now Peter had deserted him. Had little Norton panicked, thinking he'd been abandoned? Where *was* he?

Forcing himself to try and remain calm, Peter took a deep breath, and called Norton's name once again. There was a terrible silence for one long second . . . then two . . . Suddenly: *Brrrrmeowww.* Slowly but surely, a small grey head with folded-down ears poked its way out of the bush – exactly where Peter had last seen it. The rest of Norton's little body soon followed. A moment later, the cat stood on the pavement, looking up at Peter as if to say, *What's the problem?*!

Peter was so relieved he almost laughed out loud, but he didn't want Norton to know how worried he'd been – the cat had to be able to roam about by himself from time to time, after all. He quickly turned and walked home. Norton followed him at a distance all the way . . .

CHAPTER SEVEN

Fighting With Sand

Norton soon became used to walking around alone. He never did this during the week, when he and Peter were in New York – it was just too dangerous – and Norton also liked to know that wherever he went, Peter would be close by. The little cat was getting bigger all the time. He was still quite small, but his blue eyes shone brightly and his grey fur shone glossily – and he was now much more confident. Except, that is, when he was on the sand. He was terrified of it.

Peter assumed that, as he always enjoyed their ferry trip over the water, he would love the beach, but as soon as he plopped Norton down on the sand for the first time, the cat stood there shaking, then raced away for the safety of the pier as fast as his little legs would carry him. He didn't really mind where he was headed as long as it was as far away from the waves as possible.

They spent so much time in Fair Harbour, and Peter loved the beach – he and Cindy went down there at some point during every visit – so he desperately wanted to cure Norton of his fear.

He took his cat straight back to the beach again and put him down in the sand. But the moment he let go of him, Norton was gone, heading for the pier. Patiently, Peter got up and went to fetch him. But the same thing happened again and again, till Peter was exhausted from going up and down the beach.

On their next visit, he tried something different. He put Norton down in the middle of the sand, but held him there, letting the cat get used to the feel of this strange stuff beneath his little paws. He wasn't struggling, and he didn't seem too miserable, so Peter decided to risk it – he let go. Norton looked unsure, and turned his head to check how far he was from the safety of the pier, but he didn't head for it immediately. He hesitated, as if he was slowly realizing that this whole beach thing wasn't quite as terrible as he had thought. But then he saw the waves come rolling in onto the shore, and he decided he couldn't cope with it. He took off for the pier in a blur of grey fur.

But after that visit, the beach was no longer such a big problem. Norton seemed to have accepted that the sea and the sand weren't quite as bad as he had feared. Plus, he wanted to be wherever Peter was: if Peter walked down to the beach, then Norton would follow him, at his usual distance of a metre behind. He wasn't totally happy being by the sea; he meowed a lot louder than he usually did – and simply refused to go anywhere near the water. However, he'd stick around on the beach for about half an hour – especially if there was some picnic to be had! – before running back to safety.

Soon it was September: in the autumn Peter and Norton would no longer be heading down to the beach in Fair Harbour every weekend. Peter was worried. How would Norton cope with going back to being a city cat again? What would he do, and where would he play all day? The furthest he had ever ventured in New York was to Cindy's flat and back again, but even that was about to change . . .

Peter and Cindy broke up.

They and their cats had been spending so much time together that this was a big deal for them all. Cindy loved Norton almost as much as she did her own cat; Norton couldn't seem to understand why he couldn't play with his friend Marlowe any more; and Peter missed the company of the sweet little dark cat almost as much as he did Cindy.

On their last weekend in Fair Harbour, Peter took Marlowe out for a walk with him and Norton. At the end of it, he picked up Cindy's little cat and looked him straight in the eyes. "You can come over any time," he told him seriously, stroking his straight, dark ears. Norton meowed softly, completely agreeing with his master.

That night, Peter went home and cried. He was really going to miss Cindy. Norton sat down on the end of Peter's bed and looked at him, puzzled. He let Peter hug and pet him as much as he wanted, knowing that his master needed comforting. He stretched out so Peter could snuggle up to him, and they lay there for a while, Norton purring soothingly. He seemed to know that Peter found the noise comforting, so he stayed still and let it work its magic.

Things started to settle down again, but a few weeks later, Peter had a problem. He needed to go on a work trip to California. When he had originally agreed to do this job, he had assumed that Norton would go and stay with Cindy and Marlowe while he was away, but that was obviously no longer an option now they had broken up. Peter called his friends to ask them for help, but they were all busy and nobody was able to take care of Norton for the week.

Finally, Peter decided there was no other option: Norton would have to go with him. He called the hotel he was planning to stay in to see if they would be happy to have Norton along too. "Absolutely not!" was the answer. They wouldn't hear of having a cat there. So Peter cancelled his room – he didn't want to stay somewhere they wouldn't take Norton too.

He tried some more hotels, but they all said the same thing. He was getting desperate. Eventually he found the details of a new hotel that had only just opened. This was the last name on his list. He crossed his fingers and called them.

"How big is he?" they asked after Peter had told them of his dilemma.

"He's *very* little for a cat," he promised.

"Claws?"

"Yes, but he never uses them," said Peter, keeping his fingers firmly crossed. "I'll pay for any damage, of course."

The lady on the phone told him she would have to go and check with the manager. Several minutes later she returned. "Sir?" Peter held his breath. "We'd be delighted to have your cat stay with us too," she told him. "What's his name? I'll add him to the guest list."

A few minutes later it was all arranged. Norton was going to California!

They would be making the journey with Peter's agent, Esther. Esther and Peter got on brilliantly, but she was scared of flying so she was already nervous about the trip. Peter didn't want to make things any worse for her, but now that he had sorted out the accommodation, he had another issue to deal with. The other thing Esther was frightened of was cats . . .

CHAPTER EIGHT

"Get Him Out Of Here!"

When the day came for them to leave for California, Peter picked Esther up in a taxi so they could travel to the airport together. As soon as she saw Norton she frowned. She frowned even more when she saw that Norton was riding on Peter's knee – just a bit too close for comfort. "He'll behave the whole way. I promise," Peter told her.

And slowly, as the journey went on, Esther's face relaxed and her shoulders dropped, and by the time they had reached the airport and she had seen how well-behaved and adorable Norton was, she was starting to change her mind – about this cat, at least.

Although Norton and Peter had travelled back and forth to Fair Harbour so often, they had never *flown* together before, so Peter was keeping his fingers crossed, hoping that things would go smoothly – as much for Esther's sake as for his and Norton's.

They headed for the check-in desk. Peter wondered what would happen with Norton: maybe he'd have to have his own special security checks? But the woman at the desk just smiled when she saw a very cute Scottish Fold peeping out of his travel bag. She said nothing about him, so Esther, Peter and Norton carried on through security as normal.

When they reached the security gate, Esther went through easily. Peter was expecting the alarms to go off, or for somebody to say something about Norton, but they didn't. One of the female security guards patted him on the head when he stuck it out of his bag to see what was going on, but apart from that, the little cat didn't attract any attention.

Things were going so smoothly that Peter was beginning to think that people must travel with their cats all the time. This was going to be fine! He and Esther took their seats on the plane, and Norton hopped out of his bag to take up his usual place on Peter's knee. Peter decided to cover him with a blanket – it would be easier to hold onto him if he got scared during takeoff that way – then they all settled down for their flight.

One of the stewardesses walked up and down the aisle to check everything was OK before the flight, and she smiled as she passed Peter and walked on.

For two hours, Norton sat completely still on his master's lap, while Peter read his book and Esther tried to sleep. This was the best journey the little cat had ever been on – he was fascinated by all the clouds they were passing! Then, suddenly, the peace was shattered . . .

A woman with a thin, cross-looking face, who was obviously in charge of the cabin crew, walked down the aisle past Peter's seat. All at once she noticed Norton sitting there. "You've got a cat!" she screamed at Peter. He looked up from his book, Esther woke and Norton turned away from the window to see what all the fuss was about.

"Get him out of here!" the woman cried.

Peter looked around, confused. They were on an aeroplane – what was he supposed to do? "Where would you like him to go?" he asked her.

"I don't care!" she answered. "Just get him out of here."

A man in the row behind them had been listening to this exchange. Now he stood up. "There's a cat! I'm allergic to cats," he said in a panicky voice, and immediately began sneezing.

Peter couldn't believe it: Norton had been through airport check-in and security; he'd been sitting quietly on the plane for hours. Why was there a problem now? "He's been right here all this time," he told the man.

There was no answer – the poor man was too busy sneezing and wheezing to speak.

"You'll have to put him in a box under your seat," the stewardess said to Peter – but he didn't have a box with him that would fit. He tried to explain to her that Norton always travelled everywhere like this, on his knee; he was well-behaved and calm, and wouldn't disturb anybody. Even Esther joined in to defend the little cat!

But the woman wasn't listening – this was serious. She explained to Esther and Peter that it was against the law to let animals roam freely about the plane as they served food and drink during the flight. Peter was amazed: if he had done something illegal, why had nobody said anything until now? Norton was here now, and there was nothing he could do, so eventually he managed to reassure the woman by promising that he would put Norton under his seat and ensure he stayed there for the rest of the flight. To their relief, the man on the row behind swapped places with somebody else so he wouldn't be sneezing the whole way to California, and with one last dirty look at them, the woman marched away to the other end of the plane. Esther and Peter finally settled back down into their seats.

Throughout all this panic Norton had remained quiet and calm. At least, until the plane landed . . .

By the time they had got off the plane, collected their bags and found a hire car, Peter and Norton had been travelling for nine hours. As well as learning that if he ever wanted to take Norton on a plane again he needed a travel case that would fit under his seat, Peter also realized that a five-hour flight was *far* too long for Norton to go without using a litter tray.

At the airport Peter had met two other people who were going to the same writers' conference as him, so they and Esther all got into the hire car together. As soon as they did so, Norton settled himself on the back window shelf and started to mew. This was very unlike him, but there was nothing Peter could do – he was driving, and they still had quite a long way to go. Norton suddenly decided that he simply couldn't hold it in any longer: he wee'd all over the back seat. Esther and Peter's colleagues were not impressed! "Norton!" Peter tried. But he couldn't get Norton to stop. Norton kept going. In fact, Peter had never seen anybody or anything wee for such a long time!

He couldn't be cross with Norton. The poor little

cat looked miserable and kept ducking his head down as if he was embarrassed. Peter pulled into a lay-by so he could try and get Norton and the car cleaned up a little before they continued.

As he climbed out of the driver's seat, he suddenly realized that he'd been totally unprepared for this trip. He'd been selfish. He'd been so carried away with the excitement of bringing Norton with him that he hadn't taken time to think about his cat at all. He didn't have a litter tray or any kitty litter; he hadn't even brought any cat food. Poor Norton had just gone through nine hours of hell. Peter felt terrible. And he felt even worse when Norton refused to come when he called him. The little cat hid under the back seat, too ashamed to come out.

Peter quickly cleaned up the car as best he could and then drove on, stopping again at the first shop they came to. He got a cardboard box and bought some cat food, making a silent promise to Norton to treat him like a king for the rest of the trip.

When they finally arrived at their hotel, Peter checked in as quickly as possible and, having finally managed to get him out from under the back seat, took Norton up to their room. He found a couple of empty containers lying about the room, and set them up as food and water trays. Then he placed the cardboard box next to the sink in the bathroom so that Norton could use it as a litter tray.

With that all set up, he now had to put things right with Norton. Peter set the little cat down on his bed and started stroking him gently between the eyes and along his soft, grey back. "You're the greatest thing ever, you know," he told him. He kept talking and cooing to Norton, until finally the cat decided to forgive him and purred happily. They were friends once again!

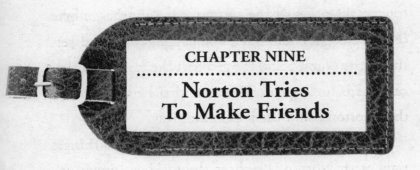

CHAPTER NINE

Norton Tries To Make Friends

Although Peter would be working a lot on this trip, he knew he couldn't neglect Norton. The little guy had already trekked across the country and had a very traumatic journey, so Peter decided to let Norton make the most of his time here.

The morning after their arrival, Peter was planning to meet some people by the pool – writers who wanted his opinion on their books. He knew Norton would want to explore, so he took him outside. The little cat was getting admiring glances from the other guests, and Peter could hear lots of "Ooohs" and "Ahhs" as they passed. He set Norton gently down by his chair. "Now go and have fun," he urged him.

Norton immediately did as he was told! He padded in the direction of the nearest set of bushes, where Peter knew he could roll about happily for hours. Just before he popped into the greenery, he turned back to look at his master, making sure that he knew where he'd gone; then he disappeared.

At various points in the morning Peter's colleagues and other guests in the hotel approached him to ask if he was sure Norton was OK by himself. "There's a very busy road nearby," one of them told him. "We've not seen him for a while," said another. "We've been calling his name for ages, but he hasn't appeared," somebody else informed him.

But Peter knew Norton better than any of these people. "He'll be fine," he told them confidently. Norton was used to being by himself in Fair Harbour – he always stayed close by.

After a while, though, their words started to play on Peter's mind. What if they were right? This was a strange place. Would Norton really be OK?

Eventually, just to put his mind at rest, he got up and strolled over to the hedge where he'd last seen

Norton and called out his name. Only a second later, Peter heard a very familiar *meow*, and his cat jumped out of the bush excitedly. Peter picked him up and kissed him on the nose, and Norton snuggled against him, happy to see his master instead of all those strange nosy people poking their heads into the bushes and calling to him.

Peter petted him proudly and then the two of them headed towards their room, Norton happily padding along behind, gazing around at all the other guests as he passed!

The rest of the conference went smoothly. Everybody in the hotel soon came to love Norton, and he was having a great time. He would spend part of the day snoozing in the hotel room and the other part exploring the hedges by the pool while Peter worked. He did attend one of his master's talks, but immediately fell asleep on top of a pile of notes, and snoozed the whole way through.

While he was in California Peter decided to take Norton to visit his parents, who lived in Los Angeles.

He called his mum and arranged to go and have dinner with them. This wasn't going to be as easy as it sounded, however. There were three problems with Peter's decision:

1. His parents' house was up in the hills and there were often dangerous wild coyotes around.
2. They had two big Golden Retrievers called Dolly and Rewrite.
3. Peter's dad hated cats.

Because of this, Peter was a little nervous when he pulled into the drive of his parents' house the following evening. He was sure his dad would change his mind about cats once he'd met Norton – just like Esther had done. Who could resist this absolutely gorgeous little ball of fluff once they'd actually met him?

Norton didn't seem to have picked up on Peter's anxiety. He had spent the drive over sitting on Peter's shoulder with his head peering out of the car window so he could see what was going on.

Peter wasn't worried about Norton jumping out – he trusted him completely – but he did get some interesting looks from people driving past! Now the little cat was sitting contentedly in his travel bag, sticking his nose out every now and then.

Peter's mother answered the door, and after saying hello to her son, she petted Norton. She hadn't been around cats very much, but she soon began to relax when Norton gently nuzzled her hand with his soft nose. There had been no sign of the coyotes, or the dogs either – so far, so good!

Suddenly, however, the friendly scene was interrupted. "Is that cat with you?" Peter's dad called from upstairs.

"Yes," he answered meekly, feeling like a little boy again.

The response was even louder. "Well, make sure I don't see him when I come downstairs!"

Peter knew this was going to be impossible – these days he and Norton came as a pair: Norton liked to be where he could see Peter and vice-versa, so Peter decided to brave it out; to try and get his dad to make friends with his cat.

Norton seemed to know what was expected of him, and as soon as Mr Gethers entered the room, the little cat gave him his cutest look. No reaction. Then he rolled over on his back with his paws in the air, inviting the man to rub his tummy. Still no sign of anything from Peter's dad, so Norton tried his next trick. He moved closer and rubbed himself up against Mr Gethers's leg, snuggling into him. Peter couldn't believe it – this was Norton at his absolute cutest – and still nothing from his father.

Peter felt a wave of sadness. Norton was so important to him now and he really wanted to get his father to appreciate how special and loveable the cat was. But he knew he couldn't force him to like his pet. Norton realized this too, and kept his distance while they ate. But he seemed puzzled. Why did this man not love him? He'd certainly tried his hardest to persuade him to.

Peter noticed that Norton was subdued on the way back to the hotel, his blue eyes serious. He travelled on Peter's shoulder as usual, but he didn't get excited about the things they passed as he normally did. Peter tried to make him understand that the hostile reception he'd had was nothing to do with him. "It wasn't you, little fellow. You're the greatest," he told Norton.

CHAPTER TEN

Surprising Dad

Over the next few days, Peter had lots of meetings. Sometimes Norton went with him and sometimes he didn't, but either way, Peter was totally happy, and so proud of Norton. The little cat had behaved wonderfully on this trip. "We should go on holiday together much more often," Peter told him one morning.

Then disaster occurred. Peter got a phone call from his office. One of his authors was asking for some major help with his book: it needed lots of re-writing, but this had to be done urgently or the book wouldn't be printed on time. The author didn't live too far away, so there seemed to be only one thing to do. Peter would go and stay with him and help with the rewrites.

There was just one problem. A very cute and fluffy grey problem. *Norton*. Peter's author was allergic to cats; and they had so much work to get through in so little time that Peter knew he couldn't take his travelling companion with him. What to do with Norton while he was gone . . . ?

Suddenly he realized there was only one option open to him. Taking a deep breath, he called the only people he knew who lived nearby – his mum and dad. Would his dad cope with having an animal he didn't like in his house for nearly a week? Peter had no choice . . .

He called his mother, keeping his fingers crossed, and to his surprise she agreed almost immediately. "Don't you need to check with Dad?" Peter asked her nervously.

But, "I think it's best if we surprise him," she answered firmly.

His dad was out at a meeting when he called, so Peter drove Norton round to their house straight away. His little cat did his cute act for Mrs Gethers again, rubbing his soft nose against her hand, and she was smiling as she took him from Peter.

Peter left quickly, almost without giving poor Norton time to meow goodbye to him. Although he hated to leave his cat and was not looking forward to his five days of hard work without him, he thought it might be better to zoom off before seeing what his father had to say when he realized Norton had temporarily moved in.

And he was right! "Things didn't go as well as I hoped," his mother told him when Peter checked in with her later that evening.

Peter wondered what his father's reaction had *really* been like; he hoped that Norton wasn't too sad or confused.

On day two, his mother seemed more positive when Peter spoke to her. Norton had apparently spent some time in his parents' bedroom and Peter's father hadn't thrown him out.

On day three, Peter gasped in surprise when he

heard his mother say, "Your father told me he thought Norton was quite handsome – for a cat."

"I'm sorry?" Peter said. He couldn't believe what he was hearing. This was the man who hadn't even wanted to be in the same room as Norton a week before. But his mother insisted it was true. Peter wondered if Norton was finally working his charm on his tough old dad.

On day four, things got even better! "Norton slept with us last night," his mother informed him.

Peter wondered if he was hearing things from lack of sleep . . .

On the fifth night, Peter was so exhausted from his hard work that he fell asleep before he had a chance to call his mother and see how Norton was. He worked on the book all through the next day and night, and as soon as he was finished – at five o'clock in the morning – he got straight in the car and drove back to Los Angeles – and Norton.

When he arrived at his parents' house, he knocked gently at the door – he knew his mother tended to wake up early. "How's Norton?" he asked as soon as he'd kissed her hello. She didn't answer but, putting a finger to her lips, led the way upstairs.

Standing in the doorway of his mum and dad's bedroom, Peter glimpsed the most wonderful thing he'd ever seen. His father was sound asleep under the covers. On his chest, on top of the bedclothes, was Norton. His father's arm was curled around the little cat, his hand resting gently on his back.

Seeing her son's puzzled face, Peter's mother led him back downstairs, where she told him what had happened over the past few days. Every day, all day, she told him, Norton had tried to get close to Peter's dad, to make the man like him. At first, he was shooed away very firmly, but the little cat refused to give up, and soon Peter's father weakened. He had even given Norton a kiss goodnight!

Peter had some breakfast while he waited for the two new friends to wake up.

Finally they emerged, and Peter tried to stop his mouth dropping open in shock. His dad was clearly besotted with Norton. "The sound of him purring is just amazing!" he told Peter. "He must be happy here. He purred the whole time."

Peter was so shocked, he could hardly speak, but he thanked his parents for taking care of Norton and the two of them prepared to leave for home.

As they climbed into the car, Mr Gethers spoke up. "Are you sure you don't want to leave him here for a while until you come back to visit again?"

Norton had won him over!

CHAPTER ELEVEN

Playing In The Snow

Peter and Norton soon settled back into their normal lives together in New York. The little cat went with Peter wherever and whenever he could, and then it was summertime, and they spent the season going back and forth to Fair Harbour again.

The people there loved Norton, and whenever he and Peter took one of their walks together, they would stop and say hello to the cat, stroking his head, telling him how gorgeous he was. Often Peter had to just stand and watch, completely ignored!

Sometimes he would ask Norton's admirers how they knew him. "Oh, he comes over to our house and hangs out with us," he was told.

He was surprised that Norton had made so many friends without him knowing, but it was obvious that the cat was more independent and much more confident about exploring places these days – he was growing up fast.

Over the summer, the cute little kitten became a much more stubborn cat! He would often stay out all night now, before returning at about five o'clock in the morning, loudly meowing to be let in. If it was raining and Norton wanted to go out, he would go out, even if Peter spent a long time telling him that he would only be wet and miserable. He just wanted to discover everything for himself.

One thing that Norton had learned had come in very useful for Peter though. By now, Peter had got himself a new girlfriend called Sarah – and Norton had played a big part in helping Peter to pick her out! The little cat had found a brilliant method for showing Peter whether he liked someone. If he approved, he would snuggle up against them and be cute, just as he had done with Peter's dad. If he didn't approve, he'd dash around and start scratching the couch; he even hissed at one woman!

But he had liked Sarah from the start, and it wasn't long before she and Peter decided to take a holiday together. Norton too, of course! They were going skiing in Vermont, and Peter managed to find somewhere to stay that would take cats too.

Norton had never been outside in the snow before. Most of his alone outdoor time had been in Fair Harbour, where there was lots of grass – and the dreaded sand, of course! But when they arrived, the little cat was surprised to see that there was snow everywhere! It was thirty centimetres deep in places and it was very soft and powdery.

Peter decided to let Norton find his own feet and see how he dealt with it. He placed him outside on the snow, but it was so high and soft that, within a moment, Norton had completely vanished! Peter couldn't help chuckling to himself as he went to go and rescue him. But suddenly, as if from nowhere, the little cat appeared again, flying up into the air, covered in snow!

To Peter's surprise, given how Norton had felt about the sand, his little cat *loved* the snow. As soon as he'd shaken off the white powder that covered him, he trotted over to the nearest tree, and then started to pad back over to Peter again. He never made it though, because he was distracted by another big pile of snow, and he dived in, digging a tunnel through the powder with his nose. He rolled around in it until he was white from head to tail. Peter had never seen him having so much fun!

After about half an hour of this, Norton began to get cold. He turned up at the door of the inn where they were staying, totally covered in snow, with tiny icicles dripping from his coat. He looked very cute – like something on a Christmas card! Peter wrapped him in a towel and dried him off, then set him down in front of the fire. A few moments later, Norton was snoozing peacefully.

After lunch, Peter and Sarah headed out to do some skiing. As usual, where Peter went, Norton tried to follow. "Stay here in the warm, Norton," Peter suggested. But Norton insisted on having things his own way. Snow or no snow, cold or no cold, he wanted to explore more of this strange new white world!

He zigzagged around all over the place as he followed Peter towards the ski slopes, climbing into trees, bounding into snow banks, and then suddenly stopping and meowing loudly when the snow got too deep – at which point Peter had to pick him up and carry him.

All in all, Norton was a very happy little cat. He loved playing in the snow and then being pampered and dried off on a towel before resting in front of the fire again – heaven!

Norton's life had become very exciting. He had certainly visited many more places than most other city cats. He had travelled in pockets, in taxis, on boats, cars, trains and planes, and had explored snow and sand – but his most exciting trip was yet to come!

Peter was working at home in New York one day when the telephone rang, disturbing him.

He was astounded when he heard who was on the

other end of the phone – this was totally out of the blue. It was a famous film director with whom Peter had worked on a book some years before. Getting over his shock and tuning back into what the director saying, he realized that he was being offered the opportunity of a lifetime. The director was inviting him to travel to Paris, in France, and work on writing a film with him.

And, of course, Norton was invited too.

Peter had recently broken up with Sarah, and he felt ready for an adventure, so he barely needed any time to think about the offer. "I'll sort out some plane tickets!" he told the older man.

Having been shouted at by the nasty stewardess on their trip to California, Peter did some research on how he and Norton should go about flying to Paris. He learned that his little cat would need some injections and a medical check-up before he could travel from the United States to Europe. Once he'd seen a vet and had these done, he would be given his very own cat passport and could travel about whenever he wanted!

So a few days later, Peter and Norton headed for the vet's surgery. The vet was a kind man, with a round, smiley face, and Norton seemed to like him straight away. He sat still and obediently while the vet looked into his ears and down his throat, and it wasn't long before he said, "All done!" and then filled in a green card: Norton Gethers, an eight-pound Scottish Fold, born in LA, living in New York, was healthy and able to travel to Paris!

CHAPTER TWELVE

·····································

The Guest of Honour In Paris

SURNAME: GETHERS

GIVEN NAMES: NORTON

NATIONALITY: AMERICAN

SEX: MALE

PLACE OF BIRTH: LOS ANGELES, CALIFORNIA

HOLDERS SIGNATURE:

· ·

A few days later, Norton and Peter were on a flight to Paris. Nowadays, Norton always travelled in a box under Peter's seat when he flew, keeping quiet and still throughout the whole journey. So Peter was surprised when a stewardess said, "Sir, please take your cat out of his case."

Peter was confused, but pleased, and Norton was delighted to find that these people who normally ignored him now wanted to be his friend!

He settled himself comfortably on Peter's lap and, when the rest of the passengers were served dinner, was treated to some salmon and milk and then some chocolate – three of his favourite things! His sandpapery tongue moved so fast it was a blur as he munched through his meal, just as if he were any other traveller.

Later, when Peter had a nap, Norton jumped down from his lap and decided to go for a wander around. Excitedly sniffing at everything with his soft, pink nose, he wanted to make friends with some more people!

When he reached the far end of the plane though,

Enjoy looking through these real-life photographs of Norton and Peter!

Norton and me autographing our book

Even asleep you can see how handsome Norton is

Norton relaxing in the country

Norton as a kitten in Fire Island. We're both happy

Norton getting ready for a TV interview

Norton on TV. What a pro!

Norton on our publicity tour

Norton at the beach, on our deck

A little rest time in our flat in New York City

Norton out to dinner in the south of France
with me, Janis and my agent, Esther

Norton at a picnic in Sag Harbour

Norton at one of his favorite inns in Pennsylvania.

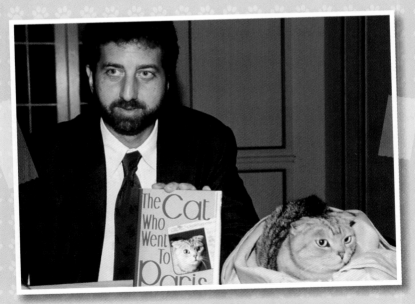

I'm giving a speech.
Norton's bored hearing the same stories again!

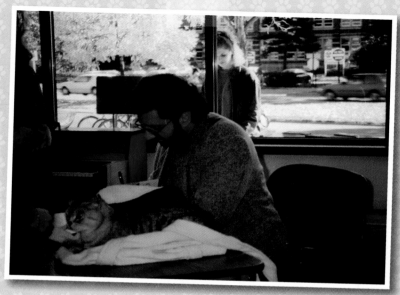

Norton totally relaxed at a book signing

The handsomest, smartest cat in the world!

he made a friend he hadn't intended to! A dog, who was travelling under the seat of his female owner, barked loudly at the sight of this little ball of grey fluff! For a moment Norton hesitated, not really sure what to do. But a steward came to his rescue. The man scooped up the little cat and carried him back to Peter.

When Peter woke and saw that Norton was no longer on his lap, but in the arms of somebody in uniform, he panicked. Immediately he began to apologize, but the man was very cheery. "Oh, don't worry, sir," he told him. "Your little cat just went to say hello to a dog!"

Norton's special treatment continued once they arrived in Paris. Even though he was spending time with a famous director, people still treated Norton like the smallest ever guest of honour! At dinner, they asked to change seats so that they could sit beside him and stroke him; waitresses would bring him little bits of fish and milk; the film director loved him; and the hotel chambermaids played with him while Peter was out for the day. Norton walked around Paris like a prince, being spoiled in the hotel whenever he wanted!

Every morning he and Peter would go to a café together and the little cat would sit in a chair, happily slurping down the water or milk the kind waiters brought him. He was able to enjoy his favourite pastime – watching the passers-by intently with his big eyes.

Back in the hotel, Norton would sit with his nose pressed against the windowpane while Peter worked. The big windows opened onto a balcony that overlooked the city, and Norton could sit there for hours, fascinated. He loved soaking up the atmosphere – Peter realized that his little guy much preferred Paris to New York. He felt the same way himself!

The writing was going well. Some days, when there was lots of work to do or Peter needed a change of scene, they would go to the director's apartment and work there. Peter had gone there one afternoon without Norton, who was perfectly happy to occupy himself around the hotel. After work Peter headed back to the hotel and was on his way to check on Norton before going to dinner. But as soon as he stepped into the hotel lobby, the manager rushed over. "Oh, Monsieur, your little cat is very sick."

Peter panicked. Norton had never, ever been sick before. And here they were in a strange country, and Norton had been ill and by himself all day. Without saying a word, Peter ran up the two flights of stairs to his room, his heart pounding. He dashed in and saw one of the hotel maids sitting on Peter's bed, stroking Norton. The little cat was curled up in a ball on the pillow.

Peter moved over to him, calling his name softly. Norton was definitely sick: he wouldn't get up to greet his master; he couldn't even lift his head. Peter had no idea what to do. As he sat with the cat, worriedly stroking his head, he made a decision. He'd wait and see how Norton was the following morning. If he was still in the same state, he would definitely take him to the vet. Peter lay on top of the bedclothes all night, watching over Norton. Every so often the little fellow stirred, and Peter offered him one of his favourite cat treats, but Norton just wasn't interested in them.

In the early hours of the morning, Peter finally dropped off to sleep. He woke in a panic. *Was Norton OK?* he wondered anxiously. He reached out for his cat and took a good look at him. His blue eyes seemed brighter and he snuggled against his master, looking much more like his usual self. *Phew!* Peter let out a long breath. Norton made it clear that he still wanted to stay here on the bed, but he was definitely on the mend.

After Norton had managed to eat a little food, Peter decided to leave him to sleep and go and work with the director for the morning as planned. At lunch time he returned, desperately hoping that Norton was still getting better.

The hotel manager caught Peter's eye as he rushed through the lobby and gave him a thumbs-up. Relieved, Peter went on up to his room – to be greeted by a very welcome sight.

Norton was lying on his back, with two maids

hovering close by and petting him. He was clearly enjoying the attention. When he realized that his master was back, he lifted his head to say hello.

Peter couldn't believe what an effect Norton had had on the staff of the hotel – they were all great friends with him, and were very concerned for his wellbeing. Peter was so proud of his friendly, loving little cat – and so, so relieved that his illness appeared to be a short-lived one. He scooped him up and kissed him on the top of his head. Norton licked his master with his rough tongue and snuggled his head against his shoulder. As much as he had enjoyed playing with these friendly maids, he had missed Peter!

The next day, Norton had improved still more, and by the end of the week he was back to his normal cheery self, wanting to set off and explore everything.

One afternoon, Peter took Norton with him to work at the director's apartment. It was a big day – one of the stars of the film had travelled to Paris to speak to them in person. And it was a big star – Harrison Ford, from films like *Star Wars* and *Indiana*

Jones. Peter was actually quite nervous; he was in a room with two very famous people, after all!

Norton seemed to realize that this meeting was important and he wandered around the apartment happily, keeping himself to himself, only stopping every now and then to be petted by Peter.

The director was talking about his film when he suddenly stopped mid-sentence and coughed; then he looked around the flat and went silent. Immediately afterwards, Harrison Ford frowned and covered his mouth and nose with his hand.

Uh-oh! Peter had a moment of realization – he hadn't seen Norton for a while, and he thought he might just know the cause of the terrible smell that now filled the apartment.

Muttering, "Sorry!" he rushed to the bathroom, which seemed to be where the stink was coming from. Just as he had suspected, there was his little cat. Norton's little grey head was down, and he was obviously embarrassed, refusing to meet Peter's eyes.

With no litter tray available, Norton had tried to

be clever and helpful. So that he didn't make a mess on the floor, he'd hopped up onto the side of the big bath – and pooed into it!

Peter rushed over and turned the tap on, still apologizing to the director non-stop. But the man had obviously seen the funny side, and within seconds he and Harrison were laughing uncontrollably.

Not many cats have the chance to poo in the bathroom of a famous film director!

CHAPTER THIRTEEN

Moving On

The rest of the Paris trip went well. Peter and the director had enjoyed working together, and Norton had had a great time too.

Back in New York, having settled into their normal lives again, Peter decided that he and Norton needed a change of home. Norton had enjoyed his freedom in the Paris hotel so much, and of course he loved his summers in Fair Harbour, but what about the winters in New York? He couldn't take as much exercise here, and as a result the little cat was becoming a big cat – he was getting fat! Peter really felt that for the sake of Norton's health he needed to find a house with a garden where his cat would be able to run about and get some exercise all year round.

Having just made this decision, Peter was invited to go and stay with his friends Nancy and Ziggy. They lived in a place called Sag Harbour, just on the outskirts of New York. It had a lot more green space than the city, so Peter thought he might take the opportunity to do a bit of house-hunting there.

Unfortunately, Ziggy was allergic to cats so Peter was going to check out their potential new home alone. He called some New York friends to see if they would look after Norton. They couldn't; nor could any of the other people he asked. Peter decided he'd just have to do what he always did and take Norton with him. It had worked out well before: Norton always managed to make people love him!

"Oh, Peter!" Nancy said when she opened the door to him a few days later, immediately spotting Norton wriggling about in his travel case. Ziggy soon emerged too, and the look on his face was not a happy one!

"He'll be no trouble, and he'll only come in at bedtime," Peter tried to reassure his friends. "He'll stay outside the whole day and just come into the house to sleep with me. You won't even know he's here, I promise."

And for the first night and the next day, the plan worked. Things changed completely in the middle of the following night, however . . .

Norton had taken up his usual sleeping position by Peter's neck. But after a few hours, with Peter snoring away peacefully, cheeky little Norton slipped away. Deciding that he wanted to make friends, and that Ziggy looked very comfortable, he popped up onto Ziggy's bed, worked his way up the covers and tried to sleep on his head!

It was 3 a.m. when Peter awoke suddenly to a strange noise. He quickly realized that his friend was shouting loudly. Racing to Ziggy's room, he immediately spotted Norton at the scene of the crime, looking rather sheepish!

"He . . . my . . . face!" Ziggy managed to splutter, pointing at the cat.

Realizing that Norton had upset their plan, Peter scooped him up and took him back into his own bed – as fast as he could!

"Come on, Norton. You have to stay here," he told the little guy firmly. And the two of them snuggled up together again, their heads on the same pillow. But only half an hour later, Peter was once more woken by Ziggy's shouts. And he had to repeat the whole performance. He just couldn't understand why his friend's head seemed so irresistible to the naughty cat!

Things finally settled down again, and Peter managed to drift off to sleep. Waking in the morning, however, he immediately saw that Norton was gone – yet again! When he made his way downstairs, he learned that his cat had refused to give up! As soon as Peter was asleep, he had sneaked back *again* in an attempt to take his place on Ziggy's head.

Exhausted, and fearing that this would go on all night unless he gave in, Ziggy allowed him to stay in the bed, gradually realizing that he wasn't sneezing – Norton was the first cat ever that he wasn't allergic to. And he was actually quite a comfortable sleeping companion! All Ziggy's annoyance was gone, and they settled down for what was left of the night.

Norton had won yet another person over!

While he was staying with Ziggy and Nancy, Peter went to meet Peggy, an estate agent, and told her what he wanted. "I have just the thing," she told him cheerily.

Peter accompanied her to look at a house. And then another. And another. And another. He dragged himself unenthusiastically around four houses, but none of them were right.

Beginning to feel slightly fed up, Peggy asked Peter to describe his perfect house so she could stop wasting their time.

Peter took a deep breath and gave her a list of the things he wanted in a home for him and Norton: old, but comfortable; cosy but spacious ... The list went on. He didn't hold out much hope that she would have anything for him.

But he was in for a surprise. "I have just the house for you," Peggy told him firmly.

And she did.

Peter knew he wanted to live in the house she showed him from the moment they entered. It was perfect — like something out of a fairy tale, with wooden floors and a beautiful garden. Peter *really* wanted it. But he knew that the biggest test was yet to come.

He went back out to the car, where Norton was waiting, his face pressed against the window. He opened the door and held his breath nervously. What would Norton make of this?

But Norton took his new surroundings completely in his stride. He bounded across the front garden and then stepped into the house. He looked a little hesitant at first, and his eyes darted about all over the place, but then he seemed to grow in confidence. He padded over to the middle of the living-room floor and lay down in the sun that shone in through the window, just as he had done the first time he had entered Peter's flat in the city. He lifted his little grey head, looked his master straight in the eye and meowed happily.

The next day Peter bought the house.

CHAPTER FOURTEEN

"Norton! Norton!"

Over the next few months things went by in a blur of happiness for Peter and Norton. They both loved their beautiful new home, and Peter also had a new girlfriend, Janis. Things went so well that she even moved in with them, and he and Norton both loved her very much. Things were going brilliantly. And then Norton had his first ever fight . . .

From time to time, Peter or Janis would notice a large, mean-looking, fluffy orange cat in their garden. He didn't seem to belong to any of their neighbours, and Peter could tell that Norton didn't like the look of him. If the little grey cat was inside when the orange bad guy came prowling by, he would stand behind the door and hiss loudly, arching his back and showing his claws in a way Peter had never witnessed before. Then he would immediately look over at his master for approval.

"Well done, little fellow. I'm proud of you," Peter would tell him, but he couldn't help being surprised every time it happened. Norton was in no way an aggressive cat. The most he had ever done was chase the odd butterfly, or meow loudly at an annoying bluejay – and even then, the bluejay often won! Peter had often tried to persuade the little cat to show the stupid bird who was boss!

One afternoon, Peter was sitting upstairs working away in his office when he heard the most awful noise. It was a wail of pain and fear, and it went on and on. He stopped still in total shock. What on earth was that? Then things got worse. Janis screamed. "Peter! Peter, come down!"

He rushed down the stairs as quickly as his legs would carry him; terrified about what he would find when he reached his little cat. He heard a barrage of violent hisses and howls, high-pitched growls, and what sounded like two sumo wrestlers thudding into each other. Peter's heart was racing and he felt sick in his stomach.

By the time he got outside, the horrible noises had stopped and there wasn't much to see. He immediately spotted the big orange monster cat stalking across the garden. His fluffy head was held high as if he was *very* proud of himself. Peter panicked. What had this beast done to his little Norton? "Oi!" he screamed at him, and waved his arms violently to shoo him out of the garden so he could search for Norton.

At first, the cat didn't even react. He just carried on without even flinching. Then he turned and gave Peter a look – a smug look that clearly said, *I could take you on too if I wanted*. Then, with one last backward glance, he trotted off into the next-door garden.

There was still no sign of Norton anywhere. Imagining the worst, Peter frantically began shouting his name. "Norton! Norton!"

Janis joined in too. "Come on, boy!"

Now Peter was totally panicked. Norton *always* came when he called him – wherever he was. But not this time. Peter spent a frantic twenty minutes searching all over the garden and in the surrounding bushes. Still no Norton. He began to feel very afraid. What *had* that big orange beast done to his little cat?

Finally he heard a feeble meow from somewhere. Peter stopped and listened . . . *Meow*. There it was again. He moved in the direction the noise seemed to be coming from. It sounded like it was underneath his car, which was parked in the driveway.

Peter threw himself down to take a look. Sure enough, to his great relief, he immediately spotted a little ball of familiar grey fur. Norton was cowering there, shaking with fear.

"Come on, Norton. Come to me," Peter coaxed gently. But it took a long time to persuade the little cat to come out from the safety of the car. Eventually, though, he managed to get the little guy to move towards him and slink out from behind the tyres.

Peter and Janis gasped in shock. Norton was

bleeding above his nose and on his right shoulder. There was so much blood that his fur was all matted and sticky. He looked dreadful, and was so frightened that he seemed to have shrunk to half his normal size.

Gently, gently, Peter picked him up and carried him into the bathroom, with Janis close behind. Setting him down in the bathtub, he turned on the water and tried – as gently as he could – to clean him up.

Norton stayed put obediently, not resisting Peter's touch, even though the cuts must have stung. To his relief, once Norton was clean, Peter could see that the cuts were not as bad as he had first thought – there had been a lot of blood, but now that had gone, Norton was starting to look better.

The little cat was still clearly terrified, however, so Peter dried him off, talking to him reassuringly the whole time.

When he was dry, Norton padded timidly into Peter's bedroom, hopped onto the bed, crawled under the covers and burrowed his way right down to the foot. He stayed there for the whole afternoon. Every so often Peter would try and get him to come out, but it was as if Norton was ashamed of himself; he wouldn't even look at his master.

A few hours later, Norton was showing more affection to Janis than he was to Peter: Peter couldn't help feeling hurt – after all, he and Norton had been through so much together. Why did he suddenly not trust him?

But as he sat beside his cat on the bed, he realized why. Norton just couldn't face him at the moment – he was more embarrassed in front of the master with whom he had shared so much than he was with Janis, a new friend.

Peter looked down at Norton and was filled with huge love for him. The thought that the little cat had so nearly been seriously hurt made him feel sick. Norton was so much more than a normal pet to him; he was his friend and his companion, and Peter had learned so much from him. He thought back on the events of the past few years. So much had changed and so much had happened, but through it all there had been Norton. And Peter knew how lucky he was to have him in his life.

A soft snoring now came from Norton, and Peter gazed at the fluffy little grey shape. He was snuggled up into a ball, sleepily happily. Giving his wonderful cat a quick stroke, Peter smiled.

THE END

ABOUT THE AUTHOR

Peter Gethers lives in New York. He wrote
his first book about Norton in 1991, and it became
an international bestseller. He has also written
lots of books for adult readers, and now works
as a book editor and runs a film company.

A WORD OF CAUTION

It's hard to meet – or read about – a kitten or a cat like Norton and not want one for yourself. Cats are very popular animals to have as pets, and they are beautiful, loveable creatures. Owning and caring for a cat can be great fun and very rewarding, but it is also a big responsibility and a long-term commitment.

If you are thinking of getting a cat, make sure you talk to breeders, vets and other owners to make sure that getting a cat is right for you and your lifestyle.

For more information about cats and cat ownership in the UK visit the RSPCA at **www.rspca.org.uk**

IMPORTANT THINGS TO REMEMBER
WHEN LOOKING AFTER YOUR CAT:

Cats need a safe environment
where they have space to rest, hide, climb,
play and exercise.

Cats should have a balanced diet
with lots of clean drinking water.

Cats need to be able to reach all
the things they need safely.

Cats should have time and space
each day to exercise so they stay
fit and healthy.

Don't shout at your cat,
it will make it nervous or scared.

If your cat likes it, try and make sure
it has **contact with people** often.

When you are away,
make sure your cat is **properly
cared for** by somebody responsible.

Never leave your cat
with another animal or person who
may harm or frighten it.

**Check your cat for signs
of injury or illness** every day.

Go and see a vet
if you think your cat is in pain, ill or injured.

Take your cat for a health check
at the vet at least once each year.

Make sure your cat's coat is kept in good condition
by grooming it regularly.

Make sure your cat can be identified,
so it can be treated quickly if injured,

or returned to you if lost.

MORE ABOUT SCOTTISH FOLDS

* It is a natural dominant-gene mutation in Scottish Fold cats that means their ear cartilage contains a fold. This is what causes the ears to bend forward and down towards the front of their head.

* Scottish Folds were originally called **lop-eared** or just **lops** after the lop-eared rabbit. Scottish Fold only became the breed's name in 1966.

* Scottish Fold kittens are not born with folded ears. The ears of the kittens that carry the gene usually start folding when they are about twenty-one days old.

* The breed was not accepted for showing in Europe for years because there were concerns about difficulties and ear problems like infection, mites and deafness. The Fold breed has not had the mite and infection problems, though wax buildup in the ears can be greater than in other cats.

MORE ABOUT THE PLACES
NORTON HAS VISITED

NEW YORK CITY

* The busiest city in the United States

* Located in the northeast of the US

* Made up of five boroughs: The Bronx, Brooklyn, Manhattan, Queens and Staten Island

* It was first founded in 1624 by the Dutch, and was called New Amsterdam until 1664

* Its nicknames are 'The Big Apple', 'Gotham', 'The City That Never Sleeps'

FAIR HARBOUR

∙∙∙∙∙∙∙∙∙∙∙∙∙∙∙∙∙∙∙∙∙∙∙∙∙∙∙∙∙∙∙

🐾 Has only one grocer and one restaurant, there is no hospital

🐾 Located to the west of Fire Island, New York

🐾 The people living there mostly do so during the summer, though there are a few families who stay all year round

🐾 Cycling and walking are the main modes of transport as car access is limited

LOS ANGELES, CALIFORNIA

....

🐾 The second biggest city in the US

🐾 Located in southern California, on the east coast of the US

🐾 It was founded in 1781 by the Spanish and did not become part of the US until 1848

🐾 Its nickname is 'The City of Angels'

PARIS

....

- 🐾 The capital and largest city in France

- 🐾 Located on the river Seine in northern France

- 🐾 One of the most popular tourist destinations in the world

- 🐾 The first signs of population in the Paris area date back to 4200 BC

If you enjoyed reading about Norton,
you might like these other titles published by
Random House Children's Books . . .

THE TOTALLY TRUE STORY OF

DEVON

The Naughtiest Dog in the World

Jon has always enjoyed a peaceful life. But when he
agrees to give a home to Devon, an abandoned little
Border collie, things will never be the same again!

From the moment mischievous Devon explodes
out of his cage at the airport, Jon realizes there's
going to be trouble. And over the course of the
next year, he finds out just how much trouble
one little dog can be!

Chasing buses, herding sheep and stealing
meatballs – read all about these and Devon's
other naughty adventures in this wonderful
real-life story.

ISBN: 978 1 849 41110 3

ROSE & IZZY

The Cheekiest Dogs on the Farm

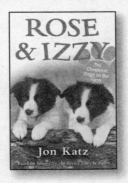

Looking after the dogs, sheep, donkeys, hens,
rooster and cat on Bedlam Farm is hard work!
But Jon is lucky enough to have Rose, the brave
Border collie always at his side.

When Jon hears about Izzy, an abandoned dog kept
alone in a field, he can't bear to leave him and agrees
to take him in. Life is just about to get even busier!
But Jon soon realizes that cheeky little Izzy
is a problem that even Rose can't help him with!

Read all about how Izzy copes with his new life
on the farm in this fantastic true story.

ISBN: 978 1 849 41278 0

Christian The Lion

Based on the story of
Anthony Bourke and
John Rendall

*The true story of one lion's
search for a home . . .*

For sale: lion cubs,
in Harrods department store!

Imagine the surprise on shoppers' faces
when they see a pair of beautiful little lion
cubs for sale in London! Two friends, Ace
and John, can't bear to leave the male cub
behind, stuck in such a tiny cage.

So they take him home with them, and
they name him Christian. But it's not long
before the cheeky lion is getting into all
sorts of mischief and sticky situations!

Whatever will they do when Christian
changes from a cute and cuddly little cub
into a powerful and noble beast . . . ?

ISBN: 978 1 862 30956 2

Look out for the
Battersea Dogs & Cats Home series!

And publishing in October 2010 . . .